HOT PLATE

ASIAN-INSPIRED BARBECUE RECIPES FROM SPIRIT HOUSE CHEFS

NEW HOLLAND

First published in 2010 by Spirit House Restaurant & Cooking School
Published in 2011 by New Holland Publishers (Australia) Pty Ltd
Sydney • Auckland • London

The Chandlery Unit 114 50 Westminster Bridge Road London SE1 7QY United Kingdom
1/66 Gibbes Street Chatswood NSW 2067 Australia
218 Lake Road Northcote Auckland New Zealand

Copyright © 2011 New Holland Publishers (Australia) Pty Ltd
Copyright © 2011 in text: chefs as per each section
Copyright © 2011 in images: Acland Brierty

A record of this book is held at the National Library of Australia

ISBN 9781742571843

Publisher: Fiona Schultz
Publishing Manager: Lliane Clarke
Designer: Fabien Barral – www.fabienbarral.com
Edited by: Helen Brierty
Photographs: Acland Brierty
Recipes: Ben Bertei, Annette Fear, Kelly Lord, Katrina Ryan
Production Manager: Olga Dementiev
Printer: Toppan Leefung Printing Ltd (China)

10 9 8 7 6

INTRODUCTION

The Spirit House restaurant and cooking school have been at the forefront of modern Thai cuisine in Australia since 1995, and were voted as Australia's Best Food Experience in 2010.

When our four senior chefs decided to create some funky barbecue recipes for summer entertaining, we were overwhelmed by the response and this book is the result.

Our three cooking school chefs and restaurant head chef have created a unique style of Asian-inspired barbecue recipes which are perfect for outdoor summer entertaining. Each chef has put their own stamp and style on the recipes and there are some truly unique gems to be discovered.

We hope you enjoy these recipes as much as we've enjoyed creating them for you.

Note on measurements
1 teaspoon = 5g/5ml
1 tablespoon = 15g/15ml
Cups: use the same size cup for all the ingredients within one recipe.
Liquid measures: 1 cup = 250ml (9fl oz)
Solid measures (vary, depending on substance):
1 cup rice = 200g (61/2oz);
1 cup flour = 150g (1lb);
1 cup white sugar = 225g (24oz)

CON

BEN BERTEI

RESTAURANT HEAD CHEF

If Ben's Dad had not made him cook the family barbecues when he was a kid, these recipes would not exist. At 14, deciding he'd had enough of barbecuing with Dad, Ben started a chef's apprenticeship.

While working on Longrain's charcoal grill, Ben's eyes were opened to the infinite possibilities of the barbecue, especially when combined with spicy Asian sauces, marinades and dressings.

As Head Chef at the Spirit House since 2009, Ben has had the opportunity to showcase his modern interpretation of Thai cuisine.

A dedicated beer drinker, Ben recommends a cold, crisp Singha beer as the perfect match with any of his recipes.

MONSTER T-BONE
with Smoked Green Chilli Relish

"There is nothing delicate about this dish. I serve it on a chopping board along with the bone for added drama - it's a huge piece of meat."

The T-Bone

1½ KG (53oz) T-BONE
order from your butcher

VEGETABLE OIL

SALT

Smoked Green Chilli Relish

1 BROWN ONION
sliced into circles

1 GARLIC BULB

300 GMS (10½oz) LONG GREEN CHILLIES

1 TBLSPN WHITE PEPPER
ground

FISH SAUCE
to taste

"Use my Smoked Green Relish on grilled meats of any kind"

T-BONE METHOD

This is a simple dish but needs time. Leave T-bone at room temperature for at least 30 minutes. Preheat barbecue to a medium heat.

Oil and salt the T-bone, place on the grill and seal both sides. Keep turning T-bone every so often for 35 minutes so as not to burn. Take off heat and rest for 10 minutes.

SMOKED GREEN CHILLI RELISH METHOD

Turn barbecue to high. When hot add onion, garlic and blacken all over. Take off, place in bowl and cover so it will steam. Repeat same process with the chillies.

Peel the burnt skin off the chillies and discard.

In a mortar, pound garlic and onion to a paste. Remove to a bowl. In a mortar, pound chillies to a paste. Combine with the onion mix in bowl. Add pepper, season paste with fish sauce to taste. Will keep in fridge for a week.

TO SERVE

Cut the meat away from the bone and slice into 1 cm (½ inch) slices. Serve with smoked green chilli relish.

GRILLED PORK SKEWERS

with Chilli Lime Salt

1 KG (36oz) PORK SCOTCH FILLET

3 TBLSPNS CORIANDER (CILANTRO) GARLIC PASTE
See recipe on page 26

2 TBLSPNS OYSTER SAUCE

2 TBLSPNS SWEET SOY SAUCE

8 BAMBOO SKEWERS
soaked in water

50 MLS (2FL oz) VEGETABLE OIL

CHILLI LIME SALT
See recipe on page 22

METHOD

Slice pork into 10cm (4 inch) thin strips then marinate in a bowl with coriander paste, oyster sauce, sweet soy and oil overnight.

Divide the meat evenly between the skewers. Thread meat over skewers using a weaving pattern.

On high heat on the barbecue, place the skewers cross ways, so the bare wood isn't over the flame to prevent burning.

Turn every 3-4 minutes until fully cooked, about 12-15 minutes.

Serve with chilli lime salt.

MINI CHICKEN LARB BURGERS

10 MINI BURGER BUNS

Burger Ingredients

500 GMS (17½oz) CHICKEN MINCE

4 STALKS SPRING ONION
sliced into thin circles

5 BIRDS EYE CHILLIES
sliced into thin circles

1 TEASPN CHILLI POWDER

1 TEASPN FISH SAUCE

1 TBLSPN SUGAR

SALT TO TASTE

1 TEASPN WHITE PEPPER

1 TBLSPN GARLIC CORIANDER (CILANTRO)
PASTE
See recipe page 26

2 TBLSPNS RICE FLOUR

2 TBLSPNS ROASTED RICE POWDER
see recipe page 56

Salad Ingredients

50 GMS (1¾oz) GINGER JULIENNE

1 SMALL RED ONION
thinly sliced

1 BUNCH MINT
washed and picked

1 BUNCH CORIANDER (CILANTRO)
washed and picked

30 MLS (1fl oz) HOT & SOUR DRESSING

1 TBLSPN ROASTED RICE

Hot and Sour Dressing

40 MLS (1½fl oz) FISH SAUCE

60 MLS (2fl oz) LIME JUICE

5 BIRDS EYE CHILLIES

1 TEASPN ROASTED CHILLI POWDER

TO MAKE THE PATTIES

Combine all burger ingredients in a bowl and slap together making the mixture firm.

Take a little of the mix and cook it on the grill. Taste, then adjust the mix with salt and pepper.

Mould to size of the buns — about 1 cm (½ inch) thick. This mix can be made the day before.

Heat the barbecue and place the oiled burgers on the grill and cook for 5 minutes on each side. Take burgers off heat.

Cut burger buns in half and toast on the grill. Put to the side.

DRESSING METHOD

Thinly slice bird's eye chillies. Mix all ingredients together in a bowl. Can store in fridge for one day.

SALAD METHOD

Combine all salad ingredients in a bowl and toss with hot and sour dressing.

TO SERVE

Place a little of the salad on the bottom half of the bun then add the burger then a little more salad. Top with other half of bun and serve.

For the Braise

3 KG (6LB 10oz) BEEF SHORT RIBS

1 LT (32FL oz) COCONUT CREAM

2 LT (64FL oz) CHICKEN STOCK

5 LIME LEAVES

1 STEM LEMONGRASS

100 GMS (3½oz) GINGER

For the Sweet Chilli Dressing

100 MLS (2¾FL oz) SWEET CHILLI SAUCE

50 MLS (1¾FL oz) LIME JUICE

FISH SAUCE TO TASTE

For the Ribs

3 KG (6LB 10oz) BRAISED BEEF RIBS

50 MLS (1¾FL oz) SWEET SOY SAUCE

50 MLS (1¾FL oz) OIL

1 TBLSPN SALT

For the Salad

2 BUNCH CORIANDER (CILANTRO) *leaves only*

2 BUNCH MINT, *leaves only*

100 GMS (3½oz) RED ONION, *thinly sliced*

100 GMS (3½oz) ORANGE SEGMENTS

1 PUNNET CHERRY TOMATOES *cut in half*

50 GMS (1¾oz) ROASTED SESAME SEEDS

50 GMS (1¾oz) RED CHILLI, *julienned*

10 GMS (¼OZ) LIME LEAF, *julienned*

50 GMS (1¾oz) GINGER, *julienned*

2 STICKS LEMONGRASS, *thinly sliced*

250 MLS (8FL oz) SWEET CHILLI DRESSING

GRILLED BEEF RIBS
with Orange, Mint & Cherry Tomato Salad

SERVES 4

BRAISE METHOD

On barbecue, char the ribs on the outside to seal the meat. In a pot bring to boil the rest of the ingredients. Place ribs in a tray and pour liquid mixture on top. Cover tray with foil and place in a preheated oven at 200°c (400°F) for 2.5 hours.

Check to see if ribs are tender at this time. They may need another 30 minutes. Take out of tray and cool down for 2 hours before grilling.

SWEET CHILLI DRESSING METHOD

Combine sweet chilli sauce and lime juice in a bowl and mix together. Add fish sauce little at a time, tasting as you go. It should taste sweet, sour and a little salty.

GRILLED BEEF RIBS METHOD

Preheat barbecue to medium heat. In a bowl, place ribs and coat with sweet soy, oil and salt. Place ribs on barbecue and slowly grill, turning every so often to get them charred all over.

SALAD METHOD

In another bowl add coriander, mint, orange segments, onion, cherry tomatoes, half the sesame seeds, chilli, lime leaves, ginger and lemongrass. Mix well then toss with some of the sweet chilli dressing.

TO SERVE

On a platter place ribs and dress with leftover dressing. Gently place salad all over the ribs and sprinkle rest of the sesame seeds over the top, then serve.

SESAME CHILLI CHICKEN RIBS

with Smoked Garlic Sauce

"You can use wings or drumsticks but 'chicken ribs' sounds cooler."

SERVES 4

2.5 KG (5LB 8OZ) CHICKEN RIBS

400 MLS (13FL OZ) SMOKED GARLIC CHILLI SAUCE

50 MLS (2FL OZ) SESAME OIL

4 STALKS SPRING ONION (SCALLION)
thinly sliced

THREE SPICE SALT TO SERVE
See page 22

Smoked Garlic Sauce

1 BULB GARLIC
charred on grill

2 RED SHALLOT BULBS

20 GMS (2/3OZ) TURMERIC

10 BIRDS EYE CHILLI
roughly chopped

250 GMS (9OZ) RED LONG CHILLI
roughly chopped

400 GMS (14OZ) TIN TOMATOES

350 MLS (11½OZ) RICE VINEGAR

125 GMS (4OZ) SUGAR

FISH SAUCE TO TASTE

SMOKED GARLIC SAUCE METHOD

Char garlic and shallots on barbecue, cook till soft. When cool, squeeze garlic and shallots out of their husks.

In a pot sweat turmeric than add garlic, shallots and all the chillies. Cook for 5 minutes. Add tomatoes and vinegar and bring to boil. Add sugar and simmer for 15 minutes. Take off heat and blitz mixture then pass through a fine sieve twice. Season to taste with fish sauce.

CHICKEN METHOD

In a bowl, mix the chicken ribs with 300 mls (10¼ FL OZ)of garlic chilli sauce and sesame oil. Marinate for at least 4 hours.

On a hot barbecue, cook the ribs in two batches turning constantly so as not to burn the ribs.

Once cooked, place ribs in a clean bowl, add some of the spring onion and remaining smoked garlic sauce and toss (and I mean *toss*, check out the picture on the right...) together.

Serve on a platter and garnish with leftover spring onion. Serve with Three Spiced Salt (see page 22).

GRILLED SEAFOOD
with Watermelon, Mint & Coconut Salad

2 LARGE MORETON BAY BUGS
cut in half and cleaned

4 LARGE KING PRAWNS (SHRIMP)
shelled and deveined

200 GMS (7oz) CUTTLEFISH OR SQUID
cleaned and scored

2 TBLSPNS CORIANDER (CILANTRO), GARLIC
PASTE, *see page 26*

1 TEASPN GINGER, *minced*

1 TBLSPN SWEET SOY SAUCE

PINCH SALT

VEGETABLE OIL

Watermelon Salad

600 GMS (21oz) WATERMELON
cut into 1 cm (½ inch) cubes

½ BUNCH MINT LEAVES

1 RED ONION
thinly sliced

60 GMS (2oz) GINGER
julienned

40 GMS (1½oz) COCONUT FLESH
Shaved - if unavailable use shredded coconut

170 MLS (5½FL OZ) SPICY CHILLI DRESSING

Spicy Chilli Dressing

3 TBLSPNS RED CURRY PASTE

150 MLS (5FL OZ) COCONUT VINEGAR

20 MLS (⅔ FL OZ) SESAME OIL

1 TBLSPN CASTER SUGAR

FISH SAUCE TO TASTE

SEAFOOD METHOD

Add minced ginger to garlic coriander paste. Rub the seafood with the paste and marinate for half hour. Then rub the seafood with sweet soy, salt and oil.

Place bugs on barbecue flesh side down then the prawns, turning once when golden brown.

Add cuttlefish — this will take the least time to cook, about 6–8 minutes. The bugs and prawns should take 8–10 minutes.

DRESSING METHOD

Combine all dressing ingredients, except fish sauce, in a bowl and whisk together.

Slowly add fish sauce tasting as you go. The dressing should be sweet, salty, sour and spicy.

SALAD METHOD

Mix all salad ingredients together lightly . Toss with dressing.

TO SERVE

Serve on a platter with the watermelon, mint and coconut salad.

"The watermelon salad is fantastic as a side dish on its own. I have featured it on the restaurant menu and it receives rave comments."

"These finishing salts are perfect for meats, seafood and vegetables. They will keep for up to a year."

Three Spice Salt

100 GMS (3½oz) SEA SALT FLAKES

10 GMS (⅓ oz) CARDAMON PODS

10 GMS (⅓ oz) STAR ANISE

10 GMS (⅓ oz) CINNAMON STICKS

Soak spices in water for 20 minutes then drain. Roast spices in oven at 200°c (400°F) for roughly 15-20 minutes.

Grind spices to a powder then put through a sieve to get a fine powder.

In a bowl, combine salt and spices. Store in an airtight jar.

Mandarin & Ginger Salt

100 GMS (3½oz) SEA SALT FLAKES

4 MANDARINS

60 GMS (2oz) GINGER
peeled and sliced thinly

100 GMS (3½oz) SUGAR

Carefully peel the zest of the mandarins and put to the side. Bring a pot of water to the boil and have a bowl of iced water ready to the side.

Blanch mandarin zest in boiling water for 20 seconds then plunge into iced water to refresh. Repeat this process once more.

Take mandarin zest and dry on paper towel then toss in a bowl with half the sugar, coating well. Place on a tray and leave till completely dry. Repeat this process from the start to the finish for the ginger. Once dried, grind both mandarin and ginger to small pieces, not a powder.

Combine salt with mandarin, ginger and sugar in a bowl then store in an airtight jar.

Roast Chilli & Lime Salt

100 GMS (3½oz) SEA SALT FLAKES

6 LIMES

8 DRIED BIRDS EYE CHILLIES

2 TBLSPNS SUGAR

Peel lime zest and put aside. Bring a pot of water to the boil and have a bowl of iced water ready to the side.

Blanch lime zest in boiling water for 20 seconds then plunge into the iced water to refresh. Repeat this process once more. Dry lime zest on paper towel then toss in a bowl with the sugar, coating well. Place on a tray till completely dry.

Heat oven to 200°c (400°F) and roast chillies for 2-3 minutes. Cool. Then grind to a powder and put through sieve to get a fine powder. Grind dried lime zest with sugar into small pieces, not a powder.

Combine salt, chilli powder and lime in a small bowl then store in a airtight jar.

Three Spice Salt

Mandarin & Ginger Salt

CHILI & LI

COCONUT CRUMBED EGGPLANT

with Soft Eggs and Black Vinegar Dressing

SERVES 4

1½ CUP JAPANESE BREAD CRUMBS

½ CUP DESICCATED COCONUT

4 EGGPLANTS (AUBERGINE)
sliced in 1 cm (½ inch) angle slices

200 GMS (7oz) RICE FLOUR

4 EGGS, *soft boiled*

1 STICK LEMONGRASS
sliced in thin circles

10 LIME LEAVES
sliced in a fine chiffonade

2 SPRING ONIONS (SCALLIONS)
sliced in thin circles

½ CUP MINT LEAVES

400 MLS (13fl oz) COCONUT CREAM

70 MLS (2fl oz) BLACK VINEGAR DRESSING

1 TBLSPN CRISPY FRIED GOLDEN SHALLOTS

For the Black Vinegar Dressing

9 GARLIC CLOVES

5 DRIED CHILLIES
rehydrated and de-seeded

50 GMS (1¾oz) GINGER

300 MLS (10¼fl oz) BLACK VINEGAR

3 TBLSPNS OYSTER SAUCE

50 MLS (2fl oz) SOY SAUCE

2 TBLSPNS SUGAR

DRESSING METHOD

Pound garlic, chillies and ginger to a paste. Add to pot with a little oil and sweat off. Add all liquids and bring to simmer. Add sugar and dissolve.

Cool mixture down and store in fridge for up to three months.

EGGPLANT (AUBERGINE) METHOD

Mix coconut and bread crumbs together. Take sliced eggplant and dust in rice flour, then dip in coconut cream, then bread crumb mix, to get a nice even coating. Place in fridge and chill for 20 minutes.

Heat flat top grill to medium heat, brush oil on grill and place eggplant pieces one at a time. Turn once the side is golden brown. Grill second side of eggplant until golden brown and crispy.

TO SERVE:

Cool slightly then arrange on a platter. Cut eggs into quarters and arrange on top.

Sprinkle lemongrass, lime leaves and spring onions over the egg and eggplant.

Drizzle the dressing over the dish then finish with the mint and crispy shallots and serve.

CHARGRILLED ASPARAGUS
with Garlic & Coriander Paste

For the Paste

8 CORIANDER (CILANTRO) ROOTS
washed and scraped

4 GARLIC CLOVES

50 GMS (1¾oz) GINGER

1 TEASPN WHITE PEPPER CORNS

10 MLS (½ FL OZ) VEGETABLE OIL

For the Asparagus

1 TBLSPN VEGETABLE OIL

2 TBLSPNS CORIANDER (CILANTRO) GARLIC PASTE

2 TEASPNS OYSTER SAUCE

1 TEASPN FISH SAUCE

2 BUNCHES ASPARAGUS

PASTE METHOD

Pound coriander, garlic, ginger and pepper corn in mortar and pestle to form a paste. Add oil and mix in with pestle.

Will keep in fridge for up to one week in a sealed container.

TO CHARGRILL:

In a bowl, combine vegetable oil, paste, oyster and fish sauces. Rub this mix over cleaned asparagus spears.

Pre heat barbecue to medium heat. Place spears across the bars and gently grill for 2-3 minutes on either side.

Be careful not to overcook.

"Garlic and Coriander Paste would have to be the most versatile and commonly used paste in Thai cooking.

It's perfect in marinades and stir-fries and is so quick and easy to make."

ROAST COCONUT AND PINEAPPLE PORK BELLY

with Mandarin & Ginger Salt

SERVES 4

1 KG (36oz) PORK BELLY
skinned - ask your butcher (keep the skin)

250 MLS (8FL oz) COCONUT CREAM

1 STICK LEMONGRASS
bruised and sliced

1 TBLSPN OYSTER SAUCE

2 TBLSPNS CORIANDER (CILANTRO) GARLIC PASTE
see page 26

½ PINEAPPLE
thinly sliced in half moons

BUTCHERS TWINE FOR ROLLING

½ CUP MINT LEAVES

MANDARIN & GINGER SALT
see page 22

METHOD

In a tray place coconut cream and lemongrass. Place pork in the tray flesh side up.

Mix coriander paste and oyster sauce together then rub into the pork flesh and marinate for at least 4 hours or overnight in fridge.

Take pork out off tray and scrape off excess marinade and place on a board, flesh side up.

Lay pineapple over pork and roll into a log. Tie with butchers twine. You might need a hand to do this.

On a hot grill, sear pork turning every 5 minutes to form a golden crust. Move to an area of the barbecue with indirect heat, close the lid and cook for 1.5 hours — if your barbecue doesn't have a lid, set your oven to 200°c (400°F) and cook for the same time.

Take the reserved skin and score with knife, then rub with a pinch of salt and oil on both sides. Cook on barbecue flat top on both sides until crispy.

Take pork belly off heat and rest for 15 minutes. Cut twine off and slice into 1 cm thick pieces. Lay on board and garnish with mint leaves and serve with crackled skin and a large spoonful of the mandarin and ginger salt.

ANNETTE FEAR

COOKING SCHOOL CHEF

Annette joined Spirit House as the first Restaurant Head Chef where she created a Thai-inspired food style that set the standard for all the Spirit House chefs who followed in her footsteps.

Travelling widely in South-East Asia for over twenty years, Annette delights in imparting her knowledge and love of Asian food through her cooking classes.

Not hidebound by recipes, Annette encourages students to experiment with flavours and ingredients, to interpret and adapt recipes to their own tastes and that of their family.

Annette's garden is her love, growing nearly all the fresh Asian ingredients that she uses every day.

BLACK PEPPER PRAWNS
with Chargrilled Pineapple

SERVES 4

1½ TEASPOONS WHOLE BLACK PEPPERCORN

4 CLOVES PEELED GARLIC

1 TBLSPN GINGER
peeled and roughly chopped

2 TBLSPNS NEUTRAL VEGETABLE OIL
i.e., grape seed, sunflower, safflower

3 SPRING ONIONS (SCALLIONS)
thinly slice the bottom half and shred green tops for garnish

1 TBLSPN FERMENTED BLACK BEANS,
rinsed and drained

3 TBLSPNS KECAP MANIS

1 TBLSPN THIN OR LIGHT SOY SAUCE

1½ TBLSPNS DARK PALM SUGAR

1 TBLSPN LIME JUICE

HALF A PINEAPPLE
peeled, sliced in half lengthways and cut into 5 mm slices

12 LARGE PRAWNS (SHRIMP)
peeled, deveined but leave the heads on

1 LARGE RED CHILLI,
thinly sliced on the angle for garnish.

BLACK PEPPER SAUCE METHOD

Crush the peppercorns in a mortar, add the garlic and ginger and pound to a paste.

Heat the oil in a saucepan to moderate heat and gently fry the paste and bottom half of the spring onions for a minute or so. Add the black beans, kecap manis, soy sauce and palm sugar and bring to a simmer, cooking until the sugar has dissolved. Remove from heat and stir in lime juice.

PRAWNS (SHRIMP) METHOD

Heat the barbecue to medium and brush with vegetable oil.

Grill pineapple until warmed through and slightly charred. Cook prawns taking care not to overcook. They should take about 5–7 minutes depending on their size.

TO SERVE

Transfer to a serving plate with the grilled pineapple, spoon over the black pepper sauce and garnish with shredded spring onions and sliced red chilli.

SOY GLAZED SALMON
with Avocado, Sesame and Mirin Dressing

For the Salmon

4 X 150 GMS (1¾oz) SALMON FILLETS
pin bones removed

1 TBLSPN KECAP MANIS
(sweet soy sauce)

1 TBLSPN SOY SAUCE

Sesame and Mirin Dressing

2 TBLSPNS SOY SAUCE

2 TBLSPNS MIRIN

1 TEASPOON SESAME OIL

2 TBLSPNS RICE VINEGAR

1 TBLSPN LIME JUICE

1 TEASPOON WASABI PASTE

1 TEASPOON WHITE SUGAR

FRESHLY GROUND BLACK PEPPER

SALT TO TASTE

½ CUP VEGETABLE OIL

Avocado Salad

2 CUP WATERCRESS SPRIGS
rocket would also be very nice

½ CUP CORIANDER (CILANTRO)

½ CUP CHERVIL

2 AVOCADO, *peeled and diced*

1 LEBANESE CUCUMBER, *finely diced*

4 SPRING ONIONS (SCALLIONS)
trimmed and thinly sliced

2 TBLSPNS PICKLED GINGER, *shredded*

SALMON METHOD

Place salmon in a bowl and coat with the soy sauces. Set aside in the refrigerator while preparing the salad and dressing.

Heat barbecue to a medium temperature and brush with vegetable oil. Place salmon on the barbecue. Cook for 2–3 minutes on each side. If you prefer the fish not so rare leave on a little longer.

DRESSING METHOD

Combine all ingredients in a bowl or blender and emulsify.

TO SERVE

Mix all the salad ingredients in a bowl and pour over half of the dressing. Divide the salad between 4 plates and top with the salmon. Drizzle the remaining dressing over the salmon and serve.

Cumquat and Lemongrass Dressing

4 TBLSPNS RICE VINEGAR

4 TBLSPNS WHITE SUGAR

½ TEASPOON SALT

2 STALKS LEMONGRASS
trimmed, bruised and cut into 5 cm lengths

2 TEASPOONS VEGETABLE OIL

1 GOLDEN SHALLOT, *finely diced*

2.5 CM (1 INCH) PIECE OF GINGER
peeled and finely shredded

8 CUMQUATS
thinly sliced and seeds removed. If cumquats are unavailable, use orange slices

1 LARGE RED CHILLI
seeds removed and finely shredded

3 DOUBLE KAFFIR LIME LEAVES
finely sliced

¼ CUP FRESH LIME JUICE

For the Chicken Breast

½ TEASPOON SALT

4 CANDLENUTS OR MACADAMIA NUTS

1 LARGE RED CHILLI
deseeded and chopped

2 CLOVES GARLIC, *peeled*

2 CM (1 INCH) PIECE OF GINGER,
peeled and chopped

1 GOLDEN SHALLOT, *peeled and chopped*

1 TBLSPN OIL

2 TEASPOONS TURMERIC POWDER

1 TBLSPN LIGHT PALM SUGAR

¼ CUP COCONUT MILK

¼ CUP WATER

4 CHICKEN BREASTS
boneless and skinless

SPICE CRUSTED CHICKEN BREAST
with Cumquat & Lemongrass Dressing

SERVES 4

DRESSING METHOD

Combine vinegar, sugar, salt and lemongrass in a small saucepan and bring to the boil. Reduce to simmer and cook for a few minutes. Remove from heat and when cool strain, discarding the lemongrass.

Put the oil in a small pan and heat to moderate, add the shallot and ginger and cook a few minutes without browning. Add the cumquats, chilli, kaffir lime leaves and strained vinegar syrup. Simmer for 1 minute and then stir in the lime juice. Remove from heat. Refrigerate until ready to use.

CHICKEN METHOD

Place the salt, candlenuts, chilli, garlic, ginger and shallot in a mortar or food processor and work to a paste. Heat the oil in fry pan and add the paste mix cooking over a moderate heat until fragrant, about 1 minute. Add the turmeric, palm sugar, coconut milk and water and cook over low heat about 10- 15 minutes. Remove from heat and cool.

Preheat the oven to 200°c (400°F) and light the barbecue, heating to high. Divide the spice paste between the chicken, brushing over the smooth side of the breast. Chargrill paste side down until very brown, turn once and cook about 5 minutes. Transfer to baking tray and cook in preheated oven for about 10-15 minutes.

TO SERVE

Transfer to serving plates, slicing if desired. Spoon the cumquat sauce over the top.

GRILLED TIGER PRAWNS
with Roasted Tomato and Lemongrass Sambal

12 LARGE TIGER PRAWNS (SHRIMP)
peeled, deveined and heads left on

4 CLOVES PEELED GARLIC

4 SMALL HOT CHILLIES
chopped

¼ CUP SHAOXING WINE

2 TBLSPNS OYSTER SAUCE

¼ CUP VEGETABLE OIL

Tomato & Lemongrass Sambal

¼ CUP VEGETABLE OIL

2 PUNNETS CHERRY TOMATOES

2 GOLDEN SHALLOTS
peeled and finely sliced

2.5 CM (1 INCH) PIECE OF GINGER
peeled and finely shredded

2 CLOVES GARLIC
peeled and crushed garlic

1 LARGE RED CHILLI
finely chopped

2 TBLSPNS FISH SAUCE

1 TBLSPN PALM SUGAR

2 STALKS OF LEMONGRASS
trimmed and thinly sliced

4 KAFFIR LIME LEAVES
finely shredded

SQUEEZE OF LIME JUICE

PREPARING THE PRAWNS (SHRIMP)

Make a paste in a mortar with the garlic and chillies, mix in the Shaoxing wine, oyster sauce and vegetable oil. Place prawns in a large bowl and mix through the chilli marinade. Refrigerate while making the sambal.

MAKING THE SAMBAL

Heat the oil to medium hot in a saucepan and add the cherry tomatoes, shallots, ginger, garlic and chillies. Fry gently until the tomatoes are starting to melt.

Add the fish sauce and palm sugar, lemongrass and kaffir lime leaves and cook until palm sugar dissolves. Remove from heat and stir in lime juice.

TO COOK

Heat barbecue to medium and grill prawns until cooked. This will take 5-7 minutes depending on the size of the prawn.

TO SERVE

Transfer to serving platter and spoon over the sambal.

For the Chicken

4 CHICKEN BREASTS, *skin on*

2 CLOVES GARLIC, *peeled*

2.5 CM (1 INCH) PIECE OF GALANGAL *peeled and roughly chopped*

2.5 CM (1 INCH) PIECE OF TURMERIC *peeled and roughly chopped*

3 CORIANDER (CILANTRO) ROOTS *cleaned, scraped and chopped*

1 STALK OF LEMONGRASS *tender inner core only, chopped*

1 TBLSPN FISH SAUCE

1 TBLSPN PALM SUGAR

150 MLS (5FL OZ) COCONUT CREAM

Peanut Dressing

½ CUP FRIED OR ROASTED PEANUTS

75 MLS (2½FL OZ) SHAOXING WINE

100 MLS (2¾FL OZ) LIGHT SOY SAUCE

1 TEASPOON SESAME OIL

3 TBLSPNS PALM SUGAR

2 TBLSPNS LIME JUICE

For the Salad

50 GMS (1¾OZ) DRIED GLASS NOODLES

2 LEBANESE CUCUMBERS, *julienned*

2.5 CM (1 INCH) PIECE OF FRESH GINGER *finely shredded*

4 SPRING ONIONS (SCALLIONS) *sliced*

6 DRIED CLOUD EAR MUSHROOMS *soaked in boiling water and sliced*

½ CUP CORIANDER (CILANTRO) LEAVES

1 LARGE RED CHILLI, SLICED

50 GMS (1¾OZ) GREEN OAK LEAF LETTUCE

2 TBLSPNS TOASTED SESAME SEEDS

COCONUT CHICKEN
with Cucumber and Noodle Salad, Peanut & Sesame Dressing

SERVES 4

PREPARE THE CHICKEN

Combine the garlic, galangal, turmeric, coriander roots and lemongrass in a mortar and pound to a smooth paste. Mix in the fish sauce, palm sugar and coconut cream until combined. Place the chicken breasts in a bowl and add the marinade. Place in the refrigerator and leave overnight.

MAKE THE DRESSING

Pound the peanuts to a paste in a mortar and then add the remaining ingredients, mixing until the sugar is dissolved.

TO COOK CHICKEN

Heat the barbecue to medium and brush with vegetable oil. Remove the chicken from the marinade and grill skin side down, for about 5 minutes or until the skin is golden and crispy. Turn and cook another 5-10 minutes until cooked through, brushing with the marinade occasionally.

SALAD METHOD

Soak glass noodles in boiling water until soft — approx ten minutes — and then drain. In a bowl, place all the salad ingredients except the sesame seeds and mix gently. Transfer to a serving platter and then spoon over the peanut dressing. Sprinkle with sesame seeds.

Slice the cooked chicken and transfer to serving plate with the salad.

CUTTLEFISH MARINATED IN GINGER & RICE WINE

tossed with Green Mango, Herb and Tamarind Dressing

SERVES 4

For the Cuttlefish

500 GMS (17½oz) CUTTLEFISH OR SQUID
scored in a diamond pattern

1 TBLSPN GARLIC
peeled

1 TBLSPN GINGER
peeled and roughly chopped

1 TEASPOON RICE FLOUR

2 TBLSPNS SHAOXING WINE

2 TBLSPNS VEGETABLE OIL

Green Mango Salad

2 CLOVES GARLIC, *peeled*

2-6 SMALL HOT RED CHILLIES

2 CORIANDER (CILANTRO) ROOTS

1-2 TBLSPNS FISH SAUCE

2-4 TBLSPNS PALM SUGAR

1 TBLSPN TAMARIND WATER

3 TBLSPNS LIME JUICE

2 GOLDEN SHALLOTS
peeled and thinly sliced

2 STALKS LEMONGRASS
tender inner core, thinly sliced

2 GREEN MANGOES
peeled and shredded

½ CUP MINT

½ CUP CORIANDER (CILANTRO) LEAVES

PREPARING THE CUTTLEFISH

In a mortar and pestle make a paste with the garlic and ginger, transfer to a bowl with the cuttlefish, rice flour, wine and oil. Toss to mix. Refrigerate while making the salad.

TO COOK

Heat barbecue to hot and cook the cuttlefish until it loses its translucency. This will only take a few minutes, depending on the thickness of the cuttlefish. Remove from the heat and when cool enough to handle, cut into more bite size pieces.

SALAD DRESSING METHOD

Combine the garlic, chillies and coriander root in a mortar and pound to a rough paste. Add the fish sauce, palm sugar, tamarind water and lime juice. Mix together and taste. The dressing should be hot, sour with a little sweetness to balance the tartness of the green mango.

TO SERVE

Place cooked cuttlefish and remaining salad ingredients in a large mixing bowl, pour over the dressing and toss gently.

Transfer to a serving plate.

SPICED CHILLI CARAMEL PORK FILLET

with Green Apple and Mint Salad

SERVES 4

Chilli Caramel Pork

2 PORK FILLETS
trimmed of sinew

100 MLS (2¾FL OZ) TAMARIND WATER

30 MLS (1FL OZ) WHISKY

200 GMS (7OZ) PALM SUGAR
chopped

50 MLS (1¾FL OZ) FISH SAUCE

25 MLS (1FL OZ) DARK SOY SAUCE

2 CLOVES GARLIC
peeled and crushed

1 LARGE RED CHILLI
chopped

ZEST AND JUICE OF 1 LIME

Apple and Mint Salad

2 TEASPOONS PALM SUGAR
chopped

2 TBLSPNS LIME JUICE

2 GREEN APPLES
skin on and finely shredded

1 CUP BEAN SPROUTS
topped and tailed

3 SPRING ONIONS (SCALLIONS)
trimmed and finely sliced

1 LARGE RED CHILLI
deseeded and finely sliced

1 TBLSPN GINGER
peeled and finely shredded

1 CUP WASHED MINT LEAVES

PREPARING THE PORK

Place tamarind water, whisky, palm sugar, fish sauce, soy sauce, garlic, chilli and lime zest in a saucepan and bring to the boil. Reduce to a simmer and cook until slightly syrupy — about five minutes. Remove from heat, stir in lime juice and set aside to cool.

When cold, marinate the pork in half of the sauce while preparing the salad. Set the remainder aside to pour over the cooked pork.

SALAD METHOD

In a large bowl combine palm sugar and lime juice and stir to dissolve the sugar. Add the remaining ingredients and toss gently to mix.

TO COOK AND SERVE

Heat the barbecue to medium. Grill the pork fillet, brushing with the sauce. Take care not to burn and turn often. This will take about 20-25 minutes to cook. Rest for 10 minutes. Then slice into 1 cm thick medallions and transfer to serving platter. Reheat the remaining sauce and pour over pork. Serve with green apple salad on the side.

GARLIC & PEPPER LAMB CUTLETS

with Warm Salad of Snake Beans, Cherry Tomatoes & Thai Basil

SERVES 4

8 TRIMMED LAMB CUTLETS

¼ TEASPOON WHITE PEPPERCORNS

4 CLOVES GARLIC, PEELED

2 CORIANDER (CILANTRO) ROOTS
cleaned and chopped

2 TBLSPNS OYSTER SAUCE

1 TEASPOON PALM SUGAR

Red Curry Dressing

2 TEASPOONS RED CURRY PASTE

2 CLOVES GARLIC, PEELED

¼ CUP LIME JUICE

¼ CUP FISH SAUCE

1-2 TBLSPNS LIGHT PALM SUGAR

1 TBLSPN ROASTED RICE POWDER
see page 56

Salad

1 PUNNET CHERRY TOMATOES
cut in half

1 CUP SNAKE BEANS
cut into 2.5 cm pieces

1 BUNCH OF ASPARAGUS
peeled and cut on the angle into 3 cm pieces

1 PUNNET OYSTER MUSHROOMS
trimmed into bite size pieces

1 SMALL RED ONION
peeled and thinly sliced

1 CUP THAI BASIL LEAVES

MARINATE THE LAMB

Grind the peppercorns in a mortar and then pound the garlic and coriander roots. Add the oyster sauce and palm sugar and mix to dissolve the sugar. Transfer the paste to a large bowl along with the lamb cutlets and refrigerate while you make the salad.

DRESSING METHOD

Combine curry paste and garlic in a mortar and pound to a paste. Add remaining ingredients and mix to dissolve the sugar.

MAKING THE SALAD

Bring a pot of water to boil, add snake beans and cook for 30 seconds. Remove with wire skimmer or slotted spoon and transfer to large mixing bowl. Next blanch asparagus, remove to bowl, then blanch the oyster mushrooms for about 10 seconds. Add remaining ingredients and toss gently with the dressing. Transfer to serving platter and serve with the grilled cutlets.

TO COOK THE LAMB

Heat barbecue to high and grill the lamb cutlets for 2-3 minutes on each side for medium rare or longer if desired.

BARBECUE SWEET SOY & GINGER BEEF

with Hot and Sour Herb Salad

SERVES 4

600 GMS (21oz) PIECE OF BEEF EYE FILLET
trimmed of fat and sinew

2 TEASPOONS WHITE PEPPERCORNS

2 TBLSPNS GINGER
peeled and roughly chopped

2 CLOVES GARLIC
peeled

¼ CUP KECAP MANIS

¼ CUP SOY SAUCE

2 TBLSPNS VEGETABLE OIL

Hot and Sour Herb Salad

2 GOLDEN SHALLOTS
peeled and thinly sliced

½ CUP BEAN SPROUTS
topped and tailed

½ CUP MINT LEAVES

½ CUP CORIANDER (CILANTRO) SPRIGS

½ CUP THAI BASIL LEAVES

2 TBLSPNS GINGER
peeled and finely shredded

2 STALKS LEMONGRASS
trimmed and inner core finely sliced

4 KAFFIR LIME LEAVES
finely shredded

½ LEBANESE CUCUMBER
julienned

2-4 SMALL RED CHILLIES
chopped finely

1 LARGE RED CHILLI
deseeded and finely shredded

Dressing

1-2 TBLSPN FISH SAUCE

2-3 TBLSPNS LIME JUICE

1 TEASPOON ROASTED RICE POWDER
see page 56

TO MARINATE THE BEEF

Grind white pepper in a mortar, add the ginger and garlic and pound to a paste. Then mix in the kecap manis and soy sauce. Place beef in a bowl, pour over the marinade and rub well into the meat. Refrigerate for several hours or overnight.

TO MAKE THE SALAD

Combine all salad ingredients in a large bowl and toss with dressing ingredients to combine.

DRESSING METHOD

Combine fish sauce, lime juice and rice powder in a small bowl.

TO COOK THE BEEF

Heat the barbecue plate to very hot, oil with 2 tablespoons of vegetable oil and sear the beef until well browned on all sides. Pull down the lid of the barbecue and cook another 10 minutes for medium rare. If your barbecue doesn't have a lid, cover meat with a large bowl or tray or transfer to a 190°c (350°f) oven for 10 minutes. Remove from heat and rest for 15-20 minutes.

TO SERVE

Slice the beef thinly and transfer to serving platter. Top with the hot and sour salad, pouring any excess dressing over the beef.

BARBECUED HOISIN DUCK BREAST

with Mango and Watercress Salad

SERVES 4

4 DUCK BREASTS

2 TBLSPNS HOISIN SAUCE

1 TBLSPN GINGER
peeled and finely grated

1 TBLSPN HONEY

2 TBLSPNS SHAOXING WINE

½ TEASPOON 5 SPICE POWDER

Mango and Watercress Salad

2 CLOVES OF GARLIC
peeled

2-4 SMALL RED CHILLIES

2 TBLSPNS PALM SUGAR

2 TBLSPNS FISH SAUCE

1 TBLSPN COCONUT VINEGAR

3 TBLSPNS LIME JUICE

2 CUPS WATERCRESS SPRIGS

1 CUP SHREDDED CHINESE CABBAGE

1 CUP BEAN SPROUTS
topped and tailed

1 RIPE MANGO
peeled and diced

1 SMALL RED ONION
peeled and thinly sliced

½ CUP MINT LEAVES

½ CUP THAI BASIL LEAVES

DUCK METHOD

Trim duck breast of excess fat and score the skin in a cross hatch. Combine the remaining ingredients in a glass dish and add duck breasts coating well with the marinade. Refrigerate for 2 hours or overnight.

SALAD METHOD

In a mortar pound the garlic and chillies to a paste. Add the palm sugar and fish sauce and mix to dissolve the sugar. Mix in the coconut vinegar and lime juice. Combine remaining ingredients in a large bowl, pour over the dressing and toss gently to combine.

TO SERVE

Heat the barbecue to medium and grill the duck breasts for about 15 minutes. Take care to turn often as the sweetness of the marinade has potential to burn very easily. If the duck is browning too quickly, turn the heat down to low. Remove from grill and rest for 10 minutes before cutting into 2.5 cm (1 inch) slices.

Mound the salad on a serving plate and place sliced duck breast on top of salad

KELLY LORD

COOKING SCHOOL CHEF

Kelly was Head Chef at the Spirit House restaurant from 2004 to 2008.

After 22 years as a chef, and sick of commuting, Kelly threw in his tea towel and started a chef consultancy company. Teaching each week at Spirit House, Kelly is also a regularly featured chef at the Sticky Rice Cooking School in Adelaide.

Much travelled through Asia, Kelly's recipes reflect his love of Singapore, Vietnam, Thailand and Malaysian cuisine. As well as sampling Asian street food, Kelly's favourite pastime is dining in London, Barcelona, Paris and New York restaurants. As a new father, will that be behind him now?

ASIAN-STYLE COLESLAW
with Lime, Coconut Dressing

The Coleslaw

¼ CUP LARGE RED ONION
(halved lengthways then cut very finely)

2 CUPS CHINESE CABBAGE
finely sliced

1 CUP CARROTS
shredded

¼ CUP CORIANDER (CILANTRO) LEAVES
chopped

¼ CUP VIETNAMESE MINT
chopped (or regular mint)

Lime, Coconut Dressing

1 TEASPOON PALM SUGAR

1½ TBLSPN CHILLI PASTE IN SOY BEAN OIL

2 TBLSPNS LIME JUICE

1 TBLSPN FISH SAUCE

⅓ CUP THICK COCONUT CREAM

DRESSING METHOD

Mix all the dressing ingredients in a bowl, then set aside for the flavours to blend.

TO SERVE

Before serving, place the cabbage, carrot and herbs in a large bowl. Toss with lime, coconut dressing ensuring all ingredients mix well.

Garnish with extra mint and coriander leaves or a sprinkle of crispy shallots if you like.

"This coleslaw works very well as a side dish to my Mandarin Glazed Pork (see page 66)."

BARBECUE PRAWNS
with Larb Salad & Roasted Rice Powder

1 TBLSPN VEGETABLE OIL

8 LARGE PRAWNS (SHRIMP)
peeled, deveined with head & tail on

Larb Salad

½ CONTINENTAL CUCUMBER
sliced with a peeler

3 GOLDEN SHALLOTS
sliced

½ CUP CORIANDER (CILANTRO) LEAVES

1 TBLSPN MINT LEAVES
torn

1 TBLSPN KAFFIR LIME LEAVES
shredded

1 LARGE RED CHILLI
sliced

50 MLS (1¾ FL OZ) FISH SAUCE

50 MLS (1¾ FL OZ) LIME JUICE

Roasted Rice Powder

2 TBLSPNS RAW STICKY RICE
also known as glutinous rice

Garnish

1 TEASPOON ROASTED RICE POWDER

½ TEASPOON ROASTED CHILLI POWDER

PRAWNS (SHRIMP) METHOD

Toss prawns in vegetable oil. Heat barbecue to a medium heat. Barbecue prawns until just cooked and arrange on a serving platter.

SALAD METHOD

Toss all salad ingredients in a bowl and arrange on top of the serving platter of cooked prawns.

ROASTED RICE POWDER METHOD

Spread sticky or glutinous rice on a baking tray in a preheated 180°c (350°f) oven. Dry roast until golden, about 15 minutes. Grind to a powder in a spice mill or with a mortar and pestle. Store in sealed container

TO GARNISH

Garnish with a sprinkle of extra chilli powder and roasted rice powder if desired.

CHARGRILLED CHICKEN
Marinated with Lemongrass & Chilli

SERVES 4

1 MEDIUM-SIZE FREE RANGE CHICKEN
butterflied (ask your butcher to do this)

100 GMS (3½oz) WHITE SUGAR

1 TBLSPN FISH SAUCE

1 TBLSPN SOY SAUCE

2 TBLSPNS OYSTER SAUCE

1 TEASPOON WHITE PEPPERCORNS
crushed

3 STICKS LEMONGRASS
bruised & bottom chopped. Keep the top parts

2 BIRDS EYE CHILLIES
chopped

1 TBLSPN CHINESE RICE WINE

1 TBLSPN VEGETABLE OIL

For the Chopping Board

2 TBLSPNS VIETNAMESE MINT

2 TBLSPNS CORIANDER (CILANTRO) LEAVES

1 RED CHILLI
Sliced

½ TBLSPN GINGER

1 LIME
cut in half

MARINADE METHOD

In a mortar and pestle, pound the sugar, fish sauce, soy sauce, oyster sauce, pepper, bottoms of the lemongrass, chilli and the rice wine to make a marinade paste.

Score all over the chicken down to the bone, to allow for even cooking and permeation of the marinade flavours. Rub marinade into the chicken and leave overnight if possible.

CHICKEN METHOD

Take the tops of the lemongrass and tie the tops with butcher's twine to form a brush.

Heat barbecue to a medium heat and brush the chicken with oil using the lemongrass brush.

Place chicken on the barbecue and seal. Turn the temperature down to a low heat and cook, with the hood closed, until the chicken is cooked through. Brush with more marinade about every 5 minutes and turn as needed - approx 30 minutes.

TO SERVE

While chicken is on the barbecue, chop fresh herbs, ginger, chilli and spread out on the chopping board.

When chicken is cooked, remove from the barbecue and place on the wooden chopping board. Cut into pieces. Rub with the chopped herbs and squeeze over lime. Serve on the cutting board.

"Lemongrass tops make a great basting brush which can be then be chopped up as part of your chopping board mix."

GRILLED FISH
with Galangal, Chilli Sambal

Sambal

4 GOLDEN SHALLOTS
chopped

1 CLOVE GARLIC

2 TEASPOONS GALANGAL
chopped

4 LARGE RED CHILLIES
remove the seeded if needed

4 CANDLENUTS
crushed

1 STICK LEMONGRASS
bruised & chopped

½ TEASPOON SHRIMP PASTE
roasted

½ TEASPOON SUGAR

½ TEASPOON SALT

For the Fish

1 WHOLE SNAPPER OR ANY FIRM FISH
approx 500-600 gms (20oz) gutted & scaled

1 TEASPOON SALT

1 TEASPOON TURMERIC POWDER

2 TBLSPNS VEGETABLE OIL

4 STICKS OF LEMONGRASS
bruised for resting the fish
on while on the barbecue.

SAMBAL METHOD

Pound all sambal ingredients together in a mortar and pestle until a smooth paste.

TO COOK THE FISH

Score fish and rub with salt, turmeric and vegetable oil. Use a teaspoon to push the sambal paste into the scores of the fish. Set aside for 1 hour.

Heat barbecue to a medium heat. Place lemongrass on the grill and rest the fish on top. Cook for approx 8-10 minutes on each side.

TO SERVE

Place fish on serving platter lined with banana leaf or some lemongrass tops. Serve with steamed rice and a salad.

"I'm using the lemongrass to diffuse the heat from the barbecue and preventing it from sticking to the grill.

A bonus from this method is that the delicate lemongrass flavour permeates the fish."

TEA SMOKED CHICKEN & AVOCADO SALAD

with Roast Chilli & Siracha Mayo

SERVES 4

½ CUP JASMINE RICE

½ CUP BROWN SUGAR

½ CUP BLACK TEA

2 CHICKEN BREAST
skin off

Siracha Mayo

½ CUP LIME MAYO
use Katrina's lime mayo recipe page 96

3 TBLSPNS SIRACHA CHILLI SAUCE
An orange coloured chilli sauce available from Asian supermarkets - Siracha is just one brand name.

For the Salad

2 SMOKED CHICKEN BREAST
cut in half & sliced thinly

2 CUPS BABY ROCKET LEAVES

1 AVOCADO
peeled & sliced

½ RED ONION
finely sliced

1 ROASTED BANANA CHILLI
peeled & sliced

"20 minutes is all it takes to smoke the chicken - any longer and the smoking mix starts to burn giving your chicken an acrid taste."

SMOKING METHOD

Place two layers aluminium foil in a baking dish. Place the rice, sugar and tea on the foil and mix together. Place a small cake rack over the foil and place on the barbecue on a medium to high heat.

When mixture starts to smoke, place chicken on the rack and cover with lid or foil. Allow to smoke for 20 minutes, then remove. If the chicken is under-cooked, place in moderate oven for a few minutes to finish. Once chicken is cooked, allow to cool.

While the chicken is smoking, take the banana chilli and roast on the grill part of the barbecue, on a high heat, until the chilli is black on all sides. Set the chilli aside to cool, then peel and slice.

MAYO METHOD

Make the lime mayo first, then stir in the Siracha sauce.

TO SERVE

Combine all salad ingredients and sliced chicken together in a bowl. Toss with Siracha mayo.

HANOI BUN CHA
with Rice Noodles & Fresh Herbs

SERVES 4

Caramel

1 CUP WATER

1 CUP SUGAR

1 TEASPN LEMON JUICE

For the Bun Cha

500 GMS (17½oz) PORK MINCE

½ CUP FISH SAUCE

4 TBLSPNS CARAMEL

½ CUP GOLDEN SHALLOTS
diced

¼ CUP GARLIC CHIVES
chopped

1 TBLSPN WHITE PEPPER
ground

For the Salad

300 GMS (10½oz) RICE NOODLES
blanched & cooled

LARGE LETTUCE LEAVES

½ CUP MINT LEAVES

½ CUP THAI BASIL LEAVES

Dressing

4 CLOVES GARLIC

2 RED CHILIES

¼ CUP PALM SUGAR

½ CUP FISH SAUCE

¼ CUP WATER

LIME JUICE TO TASTE

CARAMEL METHOD

In a saucepan combine sugar and water. Bring to boil over high heat, do not stir. Cook until the syrup is a rich dark caramel, remove from heat and add ¾ cup of hot water. Return to heat and cook until the caramel is thick and syrupy, 3-5 minutes. Stir in lemon juice. When cool store in jar in cool dark place. Keeps indefinitely.

BUN CHA METHOD

Place minced pork in a bowl. Mix through with the other ingredients and allow to marinate. Make pork mince into small patties and barbecue on a medium heat until cooked through.

DRESSING METHOD

Pound garlic, chilli in a mortar and pestle. Add palm sugar, fish sauce and water. Adjust seasoning with lime juice.

TO SERVE

Stack up bun cha on a serving plate. Arrange noodles, herbs and lettuce on a separate platter. Serve dressing in a small bowl.

TO EAT

Take a lettuce leaf, fill with noodles, herbs and a bun cha. Spoon dressing over the top. Eat with your fingers.

MANDARIN GLAZED PORK LOIN

SERVES 4

1 KG (36oz) PORK LOIN
skin off & scored

For the Brine

1 CUP MANDARIN JUICE

¼ CUP LIME JUICE

2 TBLSPNS SUGAR

2 TBLSPNS SEA SALT

1 TBLSPN WHITE PEPPER
crushed

1 TEASPOON CUMIN
roasted

1 TEASPOON CORIANDER (CILANTRO) SEEDS
roasted

1 TEASPOON LIGHT SOY

1 TBLSPN BLACK VINEGAR

2 TBLSPNS GARLIC, CRUSHED

2 TBLSPNS GOLDEN SHALLOTS
sliced

2 TBLSPNS CORIANDER (CILANTRO) ROOT
washed, scraped & crushed.

1 RED CHILLI SLICED

¼ CUP VEGETABLE OIL

Glaze

¼ CUP BROWN SUGAR

2 TBLSPNS LIME JUICE

1 TBLSPN MANDARIN ZEST

4 TBLSPNS MANDARIN JUICE

1 TEASPOON CUMIN, CRUSHED

2 TBLSPNS CORIANDER (CILANTRO)
chopped

PORK METHOD

Place pork in a zip lock bag. Pour in all the brine ingredients and seal. Lightly massage the pork in the bag to ensure the brine and herbs achieve maximum coverage and allow to marinate over night.

GLAZE METHOD

Mix all glaze ingredients and set to the side in a stainless steel bowl.

COOKING METHOD

Heat barbecue to a low to medium heat. Remove pork from the bag, place on the grill and slowly cook for 25 minutes, turning every 5 minutes.

Remove pork and plunge into bowl of glaze, turning over to fully coat. Place back on barbecue and continue to cook on a medium heat. Repeat this process every 5 minutes until the pork is firm to touch — the center of the pork should read around 80°c (180°f) on a meat thermometer.

Remove from the barbecue and allow to rest for 10 minutes in a warm place. Slice pork and serve with Asian coleslaw *(page 54)* and rice.

"The salt in the brine causes the cells in the pork to draw in the flavours of the brine via osmosis - a neat way to infuse flavours."

MASSAMAN SPICED LAMB CUTLETS

SERVES 4

Massaman Spice Rub

4 DRIED RED CHILLIES
chopped

1 POD CARDAMON
seeds only

¾ TEASPOON CUMIN

1 TEASPOON CORIANDER (CILANTRO) SEEDS

2 CLOVES

3 X 1 CM (½INCH) PIECES CASSIA BARK

1 TBLSPN LEMONGRASS
micro planed

1 TBLSPN SEA SALT

5 BLACK PEPPERCORNS
ground

¼ TBLSPN GINGER POWDER

½ TBLSPN GARLIC POWDER

1 TBLSPN ONION POWDER

For the Lamb

15 FRENCH TRIMMED LAMB CUTLETS

2 TBLSPNS VEGETABLE OIL

LAMB METHOD

Preheat oven to 170°c (325°f). Place cardamon, cumin, coriander, cloves, cassia and lemongrass in a pan and roast in the oven for 10 minutes. Add chilli and roast for a further 5 minutes or until the chilli is dark, but not burnt. Remove from the oven and allow spices to cool. Place spices in a coffee grinder and blend to a fine powder. This can also be done in a mortar and pestle.

Place spices in a bowl and mix through salt, black pepper, ginger, garlic and onion powders. Mix together and set aside in the pantry until needed.

Rub spice mix into the lamb cutlets and barbecue for 4–5 minutes both sides, or until cooked to your liking. Serve on a chopping board or platter with some of the spice mix in a small bowl.

"I'm using dry spices to make a massaman style rub for the lamb - not a paste."

SPICED TOMATO KETCHUP

Step 1

1½ KILOS (53oz) OF TOMATOES
we use heirloom tomatoes. they need to be roughly chopped

1 MEDIUM RED ONION
diced

2 CLOVES GARLIC
crushed

2 TEASPNS BLACK PEPPERCORNS

2 TEASPNS MUSTARD SEEDS

2 WHOLE CLOVES

½ STICK CINNAMON

1 TEASPN SMOKED PAPRIKA

10 RED CHILLIES
deseeded & sliced

Step 2

⅓ CUP BROWN SUGAR

⅓ CUP RICE VINEGAR

1 LIME
juiced

1 TEASPN SEA SALT

"This is REAL tomato sauce – it's easy to make and full of flavour."

METHOD: STEP 1

Place all the step 1 ingredients into a large stock pot and simmer slowly for about 45 mins or until a third of the juices have been evaporated. Stir frequently whilst cooking.

Remove from the heat and allow the mixture to cool. Once cooled, place the tomato mixture in a food processor or blender and blend on HIGH for about 1 minute.

Strain the blended mixture through a sieve and into a saucepan, making sure you have extracted as much juice as possible from the pulp.

HEATING METHOD: STEP 2

Place the saucepan with sieved ingredients on a medium heat and add the ingredients from step 2.

Allow to simmer for about 10-15 minutes. *If you prefer a thinner consistency do this step for 5 minutes.*

Once cooked, refrigerate in a sterilised jar for up to three weeks.

Kelly Lord's
Spicy Tomato Ketchup

A classic recipe. Enjoy!

CHARGRILLED CHICKEN
in Ginger, Tumeric & Cumin Paste

4 CHICKEN MARYLANDS,
scored to the bone

6 GOLDEN SHALLOTS
chopped

8 LARGE RED CHILLIES,
sliced

2 TBLSPNS GINGER
chopped

1 TEASPOON TURMERIC,
chopped

1 TBLSPN CORIANDER (CILANTRO) SEEDS
roasted & ground

1 TBLSPN CUMIN SEEDS
roasted & ground

2½ CUPS COCONUT MILK

1 STICK LEMONGRASS
bruised

2 KAFFIR LIME LEAVES
bruised

1 TEASPOON SALT

2 LIMES
for serving

"This is the sort of dish you can prepare ahead of time, requiring just a quick heat-through on the barbecue."

TO MAKE MARINADE

Place shallots, chilli, ginger, turmeric, coriander, cumin and ½ cup of coconut milk in a food processor. Blend to a smooth paste. Rub paste into the chicken and marinate for several hours in the refrigerator.

TO BRAISE THE CHICKEN

In a wok, heat the remaining coconut milk, lemongrass, kaffir lime and salt. Add the marinated chicken and gently simmer for 25 minutes. Turn several times while simmering. When cooked, remove from braising liquid. It can be refrigerated overnight if needed. Retain a little of the braising liquid for next step.

TO BARBECUE

Heat the grill of a barbecue to a medium heat. Grill the chicken for about 5 mins (or until chicken has warmed through) turning once – brush with leftover braising liquid while grilling to prevent chicken drying out. Serve with lime halves.

"The braising cooks and infuses the chicken with the Asian herbs and tenderises the meat. The five minutes on the barbecue adds a crispy, smokey crust and re-heats th chicken."

KATRINA RYAN

COOKING SCHOOL CHEF

Katrina Ryan has taught at the Spirit House Cooking School since 2001 and more recently has been a regular guest chef at the Sticky Rice Cooking School in Adelaide. Her early mentors in Asian cuisine were Neil Perry and David Thompson.

Katrina's first job as a 'real chef' was working for Neil Perry at his Bluewater Grill restaurant in Bondi. It was innovative food at the time — good quality produce quickly seared on the barbecue and served with simple yet delicious side dishes. This formula has inspired many of Katrina's recipes.

Katrina has also filmed a series of barbecue cooking segments at the Spirit House for the program 'Escape with ET'.

SPICY THAI PORK SAUSAGES

with Nam Jim

Makes 20 sausages

6 CLOVES GARLIC

6 CORIANDER (CILANTRO) ROOTS
scraped and chopped

3 SMALL HOT GREEN CHILLIES
chopped (including seeds)

¾ TEASPN WHITE PEPPER CORNS

1½ TEASPNS SEA SALT

3 GOLDEN SHALLOTS
finely chopped

750 GMS (1¾oz) FATTY PORK MINCE

2 KAFFIR LIME LEAVES
finely shredded

1 HANDFUL OF CORIANDER (CILANTRO)
roughly chopped leaves and stems

2 TBLSPNS PALM SUGAR

3 TEASPNS FISH SAUCE

SAUSAGE CASINGS (OPTIONAL)

NAM JIM Dressing

2 SMALL HOT CHILLIES

1 CLOVE GARLIC

2 TBLSPNS PALM SUGAR

2 TBLSPNS FISH SAUCE

4 TBLSPNS LIME JUICE

½ CUP VEGETABLE OIL

2 SMALL DRIED RED CHILLIES

SAUSAGE METHOD

Pound together the garlic, coriander roots, chillies, peppercorns and salt in a mortar and pestle to make a rough paste. Add the shallots and pound a little more. Tip into a large bowl with the pork, lime leaf and coriander leaves. Grind the palm sugar in the mortar and pestle and mix with the fish sauce, then add that to the bowl too. Combine the mixture well with your hands.

Put the mixture into a piping bag. Fill the sausage casings and twist the sausages into 10 cm lengths. Alternatively, shape the mixture into small patties. Cook the sausages on a barbecue flat plate using a little vegetable oil as a frying medium.

Serve with slices of fresh pineapple and the Nam Jim dressing on the side.

NAM JIM DRESSING METHOD

Pound the chilli and garlic in a mortar and pestle to make paste. Blend in the palm sugar, fish sauce and finally lime juice. Taste and balance flavours if necessary. Heat the vegetable oil in a wok and fry the dried chillies until dark and crisp. Remove with a slotted spoon, add straight into the dressing.

GRILLED SALMON CAKES
with Sweet Chilli & Ginger Sauce

For Salmon Cakes

400 GMS (14oz) FRESH SALMON CHOPPED

3 TBLSPNS RED CURRY PASTE

1 EGG

1½ TBLSPNS FISH SAUCE

1½ TBLSPNS CORN FLOUR

2 TBLSPNS CORIANDER (CILANTRO)
chopped

Sweet Chilli & Ginger Sauce

4 LONG RED CHILLIES
finely chopped (seeds included)

2 CLOVES GARLIC

2 CORIANDER (CILANTRO) ROOTS
washed and scraped

4 TBLSPNS GINGER
finely shredded

1 CUP COCONUT VINEGAR

1 CUP CASTOR SUGAR

1 TBLSPN FISH SAUCE

SALMON CAKE METHOD

Put the salmon, red curry paste, egg, fish sauce and corn flour in a food processor and process until the mixture binds together.

Remove from the food processor and mix in the coriander.

With wet hands, shape into flat cakes and place on an oiled plate.

Cook fish cakes on hot grill plate — about 2 minutes each side.

Serve with sweet chilli and ginger sauce.

SWEET CHILLI & GINGER SAUCE METHOD

Pound together the chillies, garlic and coriander root in a mortar and pestle to form a paste. Heat the paste, shredded ginger, vinegar and sugar in a small saucepan and bring to the boil. Simmer for 2 minutes and then add the fish sauce. Serve cooled. The sauce will keep indefinitely in the fridge.

WHOLE FISH
with Three Flavour Sauce

Three Flavour Sauce

6 GOLDEN SHALLOTS
finely sliced

3 GARLIC CLOVES
finely sliced

VEGETABLE OIL
for deep frying

4 LONG RED CHILLIES
seeded, chopped and pounded to a rough paste

3 TBLSPNS PALM SUGAR

3 TBLSPNS LIME JUICE

3 TBLSPNS FISH SAUCE

3 TBLSPNS LIGHT CHICKEN STOCK
(or water)

For the Fish

2 PLATE SIZE SNAPPER
or any 1.5 kg (53oz), gilled, gutted and scaled firm flesh fish

CORIANDER (CILANTRO) FOR GARNISH

SAUCE METHOD

Heat 2 cups oil in wok or pan and fry the shallots and garlic separately, until crisp and golden. Remove with a slotted spoon and set aside on paper towels.

In another pan, gently fry the chilli in a little oil for 1 minute then add the sugar, lime juice, fish sauce and chicken stock. Simmer until the sugar has dissolved. Add half the fried shallots and garlic and remove from the heat. Use the other half to sprinkle over as garnish.

FISH METHOD

Cut 3-4 deep scores in the flesh of the fish. Wrap in non-stick baking paper and then foil. Cook on the barbecue for 10 mins per kilo. Turn the fish over halfway through cooking.

Unwrap the fish and transfer to a serving platter. Pour the hot sauce over the fish and garnish with the rest of the crispy shallots and garlic.

SEARED SCALLOPS IN CHA PLU LEAF

with Coconut & Chilli Jam

Makes 20 miang

"This dish is known as 'miang' in Thai – it refers to a style of snack wrapped in cha plu leaves."

Coconut & Chilli Jam

50 GMS (1¾oz) SHREDDED COCONUT
toasted

75 GMS (2½oz) PEANUTS
fried and crushed

2 TBLSPNS ROASTED CHILLI PASTE IN SOY BEAN OIL

1½ TBLSPNS FISH SAUCE

2 TBLSPNS DARK PALM SUGAR

¼ CUP SWEET CHILLI SAUCE

2 TBLSPNS LIME JUICE

¼ CUP WATER

For the Miang

20 CHA PLU LEAVES
also mistakenly called betel leaves

1 LIME
skin and pith removed and cut into 6 wedges then across into little triangles.

20 SCALLOPS

Garnish

1½ CUP CRISPY FRIED ASIAN SHALLOTS

¼ CUP CORIANDER (CILANTRO)
coarsely chopped

1 LONG RED CHILLI
deseeded and cut into fine strips 2 cm long

COCONUT & CHILLI JAM METHOD

Combine the coconut, peanuts, chilli paste, fish sauce, palm sugar, sweet chilli, lime juice and water in a saucepan. Bring to a simmer, stir and remove from the heat when all the sugar has dissolved. Allow the mixture to cool.

MIANG METHOD

Arrange the cha plu leaves on a platter and spoon a heaped teaspoon of coconut and chilli jam mixture on each leaf. Top with one or two pieces of lime.

Season the scallops with salt and pepper and sear the scallops on the barbecue flat plate. Arrange on the cha plu leaves. Garnish with the crispy shallots, chilli and coriander.

"Cha plu is a type of pepper vine that grows throughout South East Asia. It is related to betel leaf but is smaller in size and lacks the intense taste of betel leaves."

ISSAN CHICKEN
with Chilli Tamarind Sauce

SERVES 4

For the Chicken

8 CLOVES GARLIC

3 STALKS LEMONGRASS
white part only crushed and chopped

4 CORIANDER (CILANTRO) ROOTS
washed, scraped and chopped

1 TBLSPN BLACK PEPPERCORNS

½ TEASPN SALT

1 TBLSPN FISH SAUCE

4 CHICKEN MARYLANDS

Chilli Tamarind Sauce

100 GMS (3½oz) TAMARIND

1 CUP HOT WATER

6 LONG RED CHILLIES
chopped, including seeds

4 CLOVES GARLIC
peeled and chopped

5 CORIANDER (CILANTRO) ROOTS
washed, scraped and chopped

1 TBLSPN VEGETABLE OIL

100 MLS (2¾FL OZ) FISH SAUCE

175 GMS (6oz) LIGHT PALM SUGAR
shaved or crushed

¼ CUP THAI BASIL
or coriander (cilantro) leaves

CHICKEN METHOD

Pound together in a mortar and pestle the garlic, lemongrass, coriander root, black peppercorns and salt to make a rough paste. Stir in the fish sauce and spread paste all over the chicken and marinate for at least 2 hours or overnight.

Cook over a gentle heat on the barbecue, turning frequently until the chicken is charred all over and cooked through. This may take 40 minutes or so.

Serve with steamed sticky or jasmine rice, and chilli tamarind sauce on the side.

FOR THE SAUCE

Break up the tamarind and soak it in the hot water until cool enough to rub the flesh away from the seeds with your fingers. Push the pulp through a sieve and discard the seeds.

In a mortar and pestle, pound the chillies, garlic and coriander root to a paste. Heat the oil in a wok and fry the paste until fragrant. Add the fish sauce, palm sugar and tamarind liquid. Simmer till thick. Stir in the basil leaves just before serving.

GRILLED SEAFOOD SALAD

with Vermicelli Salad & Siracha Dressing

SERVES 4

For the Seafood

150 GMS (1¾oz) SCALLOPS

200 GMS (7oz) PEELED KING PRAWNS (SHRIMP)
split in half

150 GMS (1¾oz) CUTTLEFISH OR SQUID
scored and cut into 4 cm (1½ inch) square

2 TBLSPNS GINGER
finely chopped

1 LARGE RED CHILLI
seeded and finely chopped

2 TBLSPNS OYSTER SAUCE

Siracha Dressing

2 TBLSPNS FISH SAUCE

3 TBLSPNS PALM SUGAR

1-2 TBLSPNS HOT (SIRACHA) CHILLI SAUCE

3 TBLSPNS LIME JUICE

For the Salad

100 GMS (3½oz) VERMICELLI/CELLOPHANE NOODLES

50 GMS (1¾oz) FRESH BLACK FUNGUS
shredded (or dried black fungus reconstituted in hot water for 10 minutes)

2 SPRING ONIONS (SCALLIONS)
sliced into shreds

½ CUP CORIANDER (CILANTRO) LEAVES

2 TBLSPNS TOASTED SESAME SEEDS

SEAFOOD METHOD

Toss the scallops, prawns and cuttlefish in the oyster sauce, ginger and chilli and set aside for 30 minutes.

DRESSING METHOD

To make the dressing, mix together the fish sauce and palm sugar in a mortar and pestle until the sugar is dissolved. Mix in the Siracha sauce and the lime juice.

NOODLES METHOD

Soak the noodles in boiling water and when just cooked, refresh in cold water and drain thoroughly. Cut the noodles into shorter lengths if necessary. Place in a bowl.

FOR THE SALAD

Grill the seafood on the barbecue flat plate over a moderate heat with plenty of oil.

Add the hot seafood to the noodles along with the rest of the salad ingredients. Toss together with the Siracha dressing.

TO SERVE

Transfer to a salad bowl or shallow dish. Garnish with sesame seeds.

TUMERIC MARINATED PRAWN SKEWERS

with Hot & Sour Pineapple Relish

SERVES 4

16 LARGE GREEN KING PRAWNS (SHRIMP)

½ TEASPN BLACK PEPPERCORNS

4 CORIANDER (CILANTRO) ROOTS
scraped and finely chopped

1 TBLSPN FRESH TURMERIC
finely chopped

1 TBLSPN FRESH GALANGAL
finely chopped

1 TBLSPN LEMONGRASS
finely chopped

1 TEASPN SEA SALT

2 TEASPN PALM SUGAR

1 TBLSPN FISH SAUCE

⅓ CUP COCONUT MILK

Pineapple Relish

2 CLOVES GARLIC

2 SMALL CHILLIES

2 TBLSPNS PALM SUGAR

2 TBLSPNS FISH SAUCE

¼ CUP LIME JUICE

1 CUP PINEAPPLE
finely chopped

¼ CUP CORIANDER (CILANTRO) LEAVES
chopped

¼ CUP MINT LEAVES
coarsely chopped

PRAWN (SHRIMP) METHOD

Peel the prawns leaving the tail intact. Push each prawn onto a skewer, tail first.

Place the peppercorns, coriander roots, turmeric, galangal, lemongrass and salt into a mortar and pestle and grind to a paste.

Mix in the palm sugar, fish sauce and coconut milk. Marinate the prawns for about 30 minutes in this mixture before barbecuing.

HOT & SOUR PINEAPPLE RELISH METHOD

Pound the garlic and chillies in a mortar and pestle to make a paste. Stir in the palm sugar, fish sauce and lime juice. Mix in the pineapple and herbs and taste to adjust flavours if necessary.

TO SERVE

Arrange skewers on platter, serve relish in a bowl on the side

CORIANDER & PEPPER CRUSTED TUNA

with Lemongrass & Cherry Tomato Salad

SERVES 4

For the Tuna

375 GMS (13oz) FRESH TUNA STEAKS

½ TEASPN WHITE PEPPERCORNS

1 TEASPN BLACK PEPPERCORNS

1 TEASPN SALT

2 TBLSPNS CORIANDER (CILANTRO) ROOT
washed, scraped and chopped

3 CLOVES GARLIC

2 TEASPNS SHRIMP PASTE
roasted

1 TBLSPN DARK PALM SUGAR

2 TBLSPNS VEGETABLE OIL

Dressing

2 TEASPNS PALM SUGAR

1 TBLSPNS LIGHT SOY SAUCE

1 TBLSPN LIME JUICE

1 TBLSPN VEGETABLE OIL

Lemongrass & Cherry Tomato Salad

2 STALKS LEMONGRASS
finely sliced

3 GOLDEN SHALLOTS
finely sliced

½ PUNNET CHERRY TOMATOES
cut in half

1 CUP ASIAN CRESS MIX

TUNA METHOD

Pound the peppercorns, salt, coriander root and garlic in a mortar and pestle to form a paste. Blend in the shrimp paste, palm sugar and then the vegetable oil. Coat the tuna in the paste and grill on the barbecue flat plate, searing both sides and cooking the tuna medium-rare — approx 2 minutes each side.

DRESSING METHOD

Mix together the palm sugar, soy, lime juice and vegetable oil in a mortar and pestle.

TO SERVE

In a bowl, break up the tuna into small pieces and toss gently with the salad ingredients and the dressing.

"Make your salad dressings in a mortar and pestle. This allows you to mix and grind your ingredients all at the same time."

TWICE COOKED LAMB SHANKS

with Massaman Paste and Coconut Salad

SERVES 4

4 LAMB SHANKS
Braise the lamb shanks the day before.

500 MLS (16FL OZ) COCONUT CREAM

1 TBLSPN FISH SAUCE

1 TBLSPN PALM SUGAR

2 CUPS WATER

For the Barbecue Lamb

4 TBLSPNS MASSAMAN CURRY PASTE

4 TBLSPNS KECAP MANIS

VEGETABLE OIL
for cooking

For the Dressing

½ CUP COCONUT VINEGAR

½ CUP CASTOR SUGAR

Coconut Salad

2 LEBANESE CUCUMBERS
halved and sliced on the diagonal

½ FRESH COCONUT GRATED

1 GREEN SHALLOT
finely sliced on the diagonal

2 GOLDEN SHALLOTS
finely sliced

1 CUP CORIANDER (CILANTRO) LEAVES

1 CUP MINT LEAVES

2 LONG RED CHILLIES
deseeded and cut into fine julienne

½ CUP FRIED PEANUTS
roughly chopped

"Braising the lamb shanks not only flavours the meat it also makes the lamb incredibly tender. This dish simply melts in your mouth."

BRAISING LAMB SHANKS METHOD

Put the lamb shanks in a baking dish with the coconut cream, fish sauce, palm sugar and water. Cover with a lid or foil and bake at 150-160°c (300°f) for 2½ hours until tender. Cool in the stock. Remove the shanks and refrigerate until ready to cook.

BARBECUE METHOD

Coat the lamb shanks in the curry paste and kecap manis. Oil the barbecue flat plate well and cook the lamb shanks all over until lightly charred and heated through.

DRESSING METHOD

Boil the vinegar and sugar together for 1 minute then add the fish sauce. Cool.

TO SERVE

Toss the salad ingredients with the dressing and serve with the hot shanks.

LAMB CUTLETS MARINATED WITH RED BEAN CURD

Spicy Eggplant Relish

SERVES 4

For the Lamb

12 LAMB CUTLETS

For the Marinade

3 TBLSPNS FERMENTED RED BEAN CURD

1 TBLSPN CHILLI BEAN SAUCE

3 TBLSPNS SOY SAUCE

1 TBLSPN SESAME OIL

1 TBLSPN SHAOXING WINE

3 TBLSPNS SUGAR

Spicy Eggplant Relish

1 LARGE EGGPLANT (AUBERGINE)
*cut into 2 cm slices (¾ inch) (quite thick)
and lightly salt for 20 minutes*

ABOUT ¾ CUP PEANUT OIL
for frying

1 TBLSPN LAKSA PASTE
or red curry paste

4 TBLSPNS CASTOR SUGAR

3 TBLSPNS RICE VINEGAR

¼ CUP CORIANDER (CILANTRO) LEAVES
chopped

LAMB CUTLET METHOD

Combine the marinade ingredients and coat the lamb. Marinate overnight if possible. Grill on the barbecue flat plate until medium rare. Rest the cutlets for 5 minutes. Serve on a bed of lettuce with the relish on the side.

EGGPLANT (AUBERGINE) RELISH METHOD

Pat dry the eggplant. In a pan, heat the oil until very hot and fry the eggplant slices until well browned on both sides. Remove to a bowl once they are cooked.

When the last piece of eggplant has been removed from the pan, lower the heat, add the laksa paste and fry for one minute. Add the sugar and vinegar and cook until it becomes syrupy.

Pour over the eggplant and add the coriander as well. Chop and stir gently with a spoon to combine and break up the eggplant without turning it to mush.

It may be stored in the refrigerator for up to a month.

MAYONNAISE

"These are easy to make and much nicer than store-bought mayos. Keeps 3-4 weeks in a refrigerator."

Lime Mayo

1 EGG YOLK

1 TEASPN DIJON MUSTARD

1 TEASPN SEA SALT

JUICE 1 LIME

1 TEASPN CASTOR SUGAR

1 CUP EXTRA LIGHT OLIVE OIL

Put the egg yolk, mustard, salt, lime juice and sugar into a bowl and mix well with a whisk. (Or use a hand held Bamix and jug)

Slowly add the oil, drop by drop at first and whisking constantly, to ensure emulsification. As the mayonnaise thickens, add the oil in a thin stream. If it gets very thick, add a little water to thin to desired consistency.

Wasabi Mayo

1 EGG YOLK

1 TEASPN DIJON MUSTARD

½ TEASPN SEA SALT

3 TEASPNS JAPANESE RICE VINEGAR

2 TEASPNS CASTOR SUGAR

3 TEASPNS PREPARED WASABI

¾ CUP RICE BRAN OR PEANUT OIL

Put the egg yolk, mustard, salt, vinegar, sugar and wasabi into a bowl and mix well with a whisk. (Or use a hand held Bamix and jug)

Slowly add the oil, drop by drop at first and whisking constantly, to ensure emulsification. As the mayonnaise thickens, add the oil in a thin stream. If it gets very thick, add a little water to thin to desired consistency.

Garlic Mayo

1 CLOVE GARLIC

1 EGG YOLK

1 TEASPN DIJON MUSTARD

1 TEASPN SEA SALT

1½ TBLSPNS WHITE BALSAMIC VINEGAR

1 CUP EXTRA LIGHT OLIVE OIL

Put the garlic, egg yolk, mustard, salt and vinegar into a bowl and mix well with a whisk. (Or use a hand held Bamix and jug)

Slowly add the oil, drop by drop at first and whisking constantly, to ensure emulsification. As the mayonnaise thickens, add the oil in a thin stream. If it gets very thick, add a little water to thin to desired consistency.

CROSTINI

with Prawns, Chilli, Mint

1 BAGUETTE LOAF

EXTRA VIRGIN OLIVE OIL
for brushing the bread

750 GMS (1¾oz) FRESH COOKED PRAWNS (SHRIMP)
peeled, deveined and chopped

¼ CUP CHOPPED FRESH MINT

1 LIME
skin removed and cut into slices

2 SMALL HOT CHILLIES
finely chopped

2 TBLSPN EXTRA VIRGIN OLIVE OIL

2 TEASPN WHITE BALSAMIC VINEGAR

PEPPER TO TASTE

LIME MAYO
see previous page

with Pepper Crusted Tuna

1 BAGUETTE LOAF

EXTRA VIRGIN OLIVE OIL
for brushing the bread

400 GMS (14oz) PEPPER CRUSTED TUNA
see recipe page 96

2 TBLSPNS PICKLED GINGER

½ CUP CORIANDER (CILANTRO) LEAVES

WASABI MAYO
see previous page

with Smoked Salmon

1 BAGUETTE LOAF

250 GMS (1¾oz) SMOKED SALMON
or gravlax

EXTRA VIRGIN OLIVE OIL
for brushing the bread

2 GOLDEN SHALLOTS FINELY DICED

4 RIPE TOMATOES FINELY CHOPPED

2 TBLSPNS CHIVES
finely chopped

2 TBLSPNS TOASTED SESAME SEEDS

2 TBLSPNS EXTRA VIRGIN OLIVE OIL

1 TBLSPN LEMON JUICE

SALT AND PEPPER TO TASTE

GARLIC MAYO
see previous page

Cut the bread into thick slices and set aside. Place prawns in a bowl with the fresh mint, chilli, lime, oil, vinegar and salt and pepper to taste. Toss well.

Brush the bread with oil both sides and grill on the barbecue.

Spread with the lime mayonnaise and top with the prawn mixture. Serve immediately.

Cut the bread into thick slices and set aside. Slice tuna thinly. Brush the bread with oil both sides and grill on the barbecue.

Spread with the wasabi mayonnaise and place a piece of tuna on top followed by coriander leaves and a little pickled ginger.

Serve immediately.

Cut the bread into thick slices and set aside. Make a salsa by combining the shallots, tomatoes, chives, sesame seeds, olive oil, lemon juice and salt and pepper.

Brush the bread with oil both sides and grill on the barbecue.

Top the bread with the garlic mayonnaise, then the sliced salmon and then a dollop of the salsa.

INDEX »

HOT TIPS

FOR BEST RESULTS

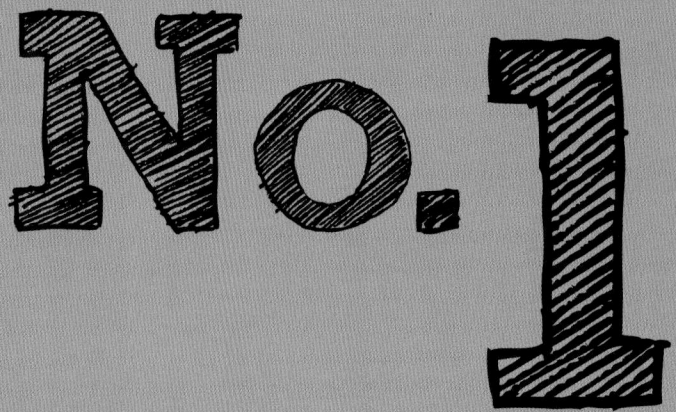

No.1

REST THE MEAT

Resting meat for 5-10 minutes after it has been cooked allows the meat to relax. The juices then redistribute throughout and thus the meat becomes more tender.

Interestingly, the meat will continue to cook while it's resting thanks to the residual heat - so don't think your steak will go cold if you let it rest.

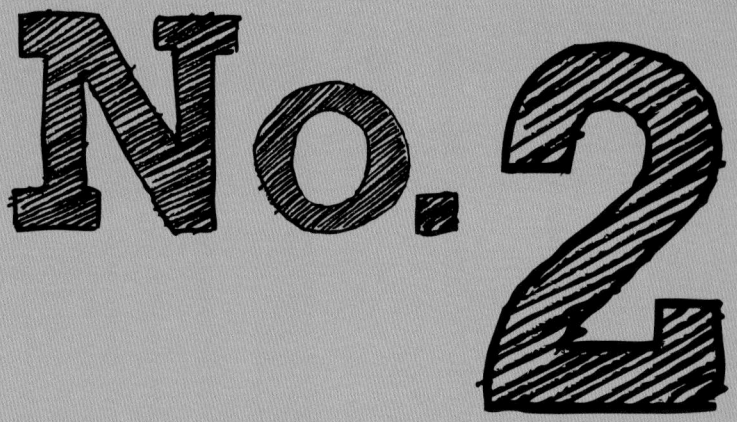

No.2

BE PREPARED

Professional chefs spend hours chopping and prepping their ingredients before a restaurant service begins.

(Actually, they have apprentices doing their chopping.)

You probably don't have an apprentice, so before you put anything on the barbecue, have everything prepped and ready - including the salads.

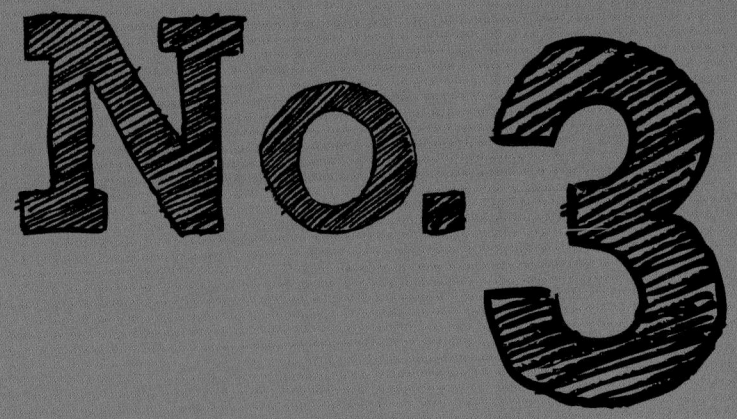

No.3

A SHARP KNIFE

The difference between a chef's knife and your knife at home is that chef's knife is always SHARP.

Treat your knife with respect and have it professionally sharpened. Steeling your knife maintains the edge, but won't sharpen it.

Do not put your knife in a dishwasher. The buffeting in the wash cycle takes the fine edge off the blade.

Likewise, do not store your knife in a kitchen drawer because the blade gets knocked around - invest in a magnetic knife holder.

A

ASPARAGUS
Chargrilled Asparagus with Garlic & Coriander Paste   26

AUBERGINE (SEE EGGPLANT)

B

BEEF
Barbecue Sweet Soy & Ginger Beef with Hot and Sour Herb Salad   48

Grilled Beef Ribs with Orange, Mint & Cherry Tomato Salad   16

Monster T-Bone with Smoked Green Chilli Relish   10

BETEL LEAF   82

BRINE   66

BUN CHA WITH RICE NOODLES & FRESH HERBS   64

C

CARAMEL   64

CHICKEN
Chargrilled Chicken Marinated with Lemongrass & Chilli   58

Coconut Chicken with Cucumber and Noodle Salad, Peanut & Sesame Dressing   40

Issan Chicken with Chilli Tamarind Sauce   84

Mini Chicken Larb Burgers   14

Sesame Chilli Chicken Ribs with Smoked Garlic Sauce   18

Spice Crusted Chicken Breast with Cumquat & Lemongrass Dressing   36

Tea Smoked Chicken & Avocado Salad with Roast Chilli & Siracha Mayo   62

Chargrilled Chicken with Ginger, Tumeric & Cumin Paste   72

CHILANTRO (SEE CORIANDER)

COCONUT & CHILLI JAM   82

CORIANDER & GINGER DIPPING SAUCE   72

CROSTINI
with Pepper Crusted Tuna   98

with Prawns, Chilli, Mint   98

with Smoked Salmon   98

CUTTLEFISH
Cuttlefish Marinated in Ginger & Rice Wine   42

D

DIPPING SAUCES
Coriander & Ginger Dipping Sauce   72

DRESSINGS
Avocado, Sesame and Mirin Dressing   34

Black Vinegar Dressing   24

Cumquat & Lemongrass Dressing   36

Herb and Tamarind Dressing   42

Hot and Sour Dressing   14

Lime, Coconut Dressing   54

Peanut & Sesame Dressing   40

Red Curry Dressing   46

Siracha Dressing   86

Spicy Chilli Dressing   20

Sweet Chilli Dressing   16

DUCK
Barbecued Hoisin Duck Breast with Mango and Watercress Salad   50

E

EGGPLANT (AUBERGINE)
Coconut Crumbed Eggplant with Soft Eggs and Black Vinegar Dressing   24

Spicy Eggplant Relish   94

F

FISH
Grilled Salmon Cakes with Sweet Chilli & Ginger Sauce   78

Grilled Snapper with Galangal, Chilli Sambal   60

Smoked Salmon   98

Soy Glazed Salmon with Avocado, Sesame and Mirin Dressing

Whole Snapper with Three Flavour Sauce   80

Coriander & Pepper Crusted Tuna with Lemongrass & Cherry Tomato Salad   90

FLAVOURING SALTS   22

G

GARLIC & CORIANDER PASTE   26

L

LAMB
Garlic & Pepper Lamb Cutlets with Warm Salad of Snake Beans, Cherry Tomatoes & Thai Basil   46

Lamb Cutlets Marinated with Red Bean Curd

Spicy Eggplant Relish   94

Massaman Spiced Lamb Cutlets   68

Twice Cooked Lamb Shanks with Massaman Paste and Coconut Salad   92

Look for these other Spirit House titles from New Holland

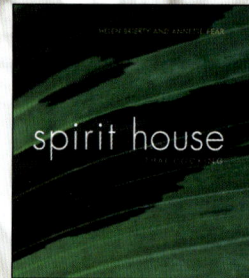

SPIRIT HOUSE RESTAURANT & COOKING SCHOOL
20 Ninderry Rd • Yandina • Qld • 4561
AUSTRALIA

CONTACT US:
www.spirithouse.com.au | EMAIL: ADMIN@SPIRITHOUSE.COM.AU